MW01436605

~~WHITMAN MIDDLE SCHOOL LIBRARY~~

DALAI LAMA: Spiritual Leader of Tibet

I am an ordinary Buddhist monk. My religion is kindness, and my heart is my people.
—The Dalai Lama

Mason Crest
450 Parkway Drive, Suite D
Broomall, PA 19008
www.masoncrest.com

Copyright © 2014 by Mason Crest, an imprint of National Highlights, Inc. All rights reserved. No part of this publication may be reproduced or transmitted in any form or by any means, electronic or mechanical, including photocopying, recording, taping or any information storage and retrieval system, without permission from the publisher.

Printed and bound in the United States of America.

First printing
9 8 7 6 5 4 3 2 1

Series ISBN: 978-1-4222-2839-5
ISBN: 978-1-4222-2846-3
ebook ISBN: 978-1-4222-8966-2

The Library of Congress has cataloged the hardcopy format(s) as follows:

Library of Congress Cataloging-in-Publication Data

Sullivan, Anne Marie.
  Dalai Lama : Spiritual Leader of Tibet / Anne Marie Sullivan.
    pages cm. — (People of Importance)
  ISBN 978-1-4222-2846-3 (hardcover) — ISBN 978-1-4222-2839-5 (series) — ISBN 978-1-4222-8966-2 (ebook)
  1. Bstan-'dzin-rgya-mtsho, Dalai Lama XIV, 1935—Juvenile literature. 2. Dalai lamas—Biography—Juvenile literature. I. Title.
  BQ7935.B777S85 2014
  294.3'923092—dc23
    [B]
                                                2013006364

Produced by Vestal Creative Services.
www.vestalcreative.com
Illustrations copyright © 2000 Chen Jian-jiang.

People of Importance

DALAI LAMA: Spiritual Leader of Tibet

Anne Marie Sullivan   Chen Jian-Jiang

Mason Crest

Once upon a time, in the seventh century, there lived a powerful king in the high mountains of Tibet. His name was Song Tsen Gampo. A strong and skillful warrior, he spread the borders of his kingdom until it stretched into India and China. This king married two wives, one a princess of Nepal, the other a princess of China. Both wives faithfully followed the teachings of the Buddha, who showed his followers the path to wisdom through love and kindness.

Song Tsen Gampo fell in love with his Chinese wife, the Princess Wen Cheng, while meeting with her father, the Chinese emperor. He offered the emperor gold and treasure in exchange for her hand in marriage. The emperor hesitated. He was not sure that he wanted to send the daughter he loved to a strange land. But he finally agreed, wishing to make peace with the Tibetan king.

Reluctantly, Wen Cheng obeyed her father's wish, crossing high mountains and vast deserts in a camel caravan to join her groom in Tibet.

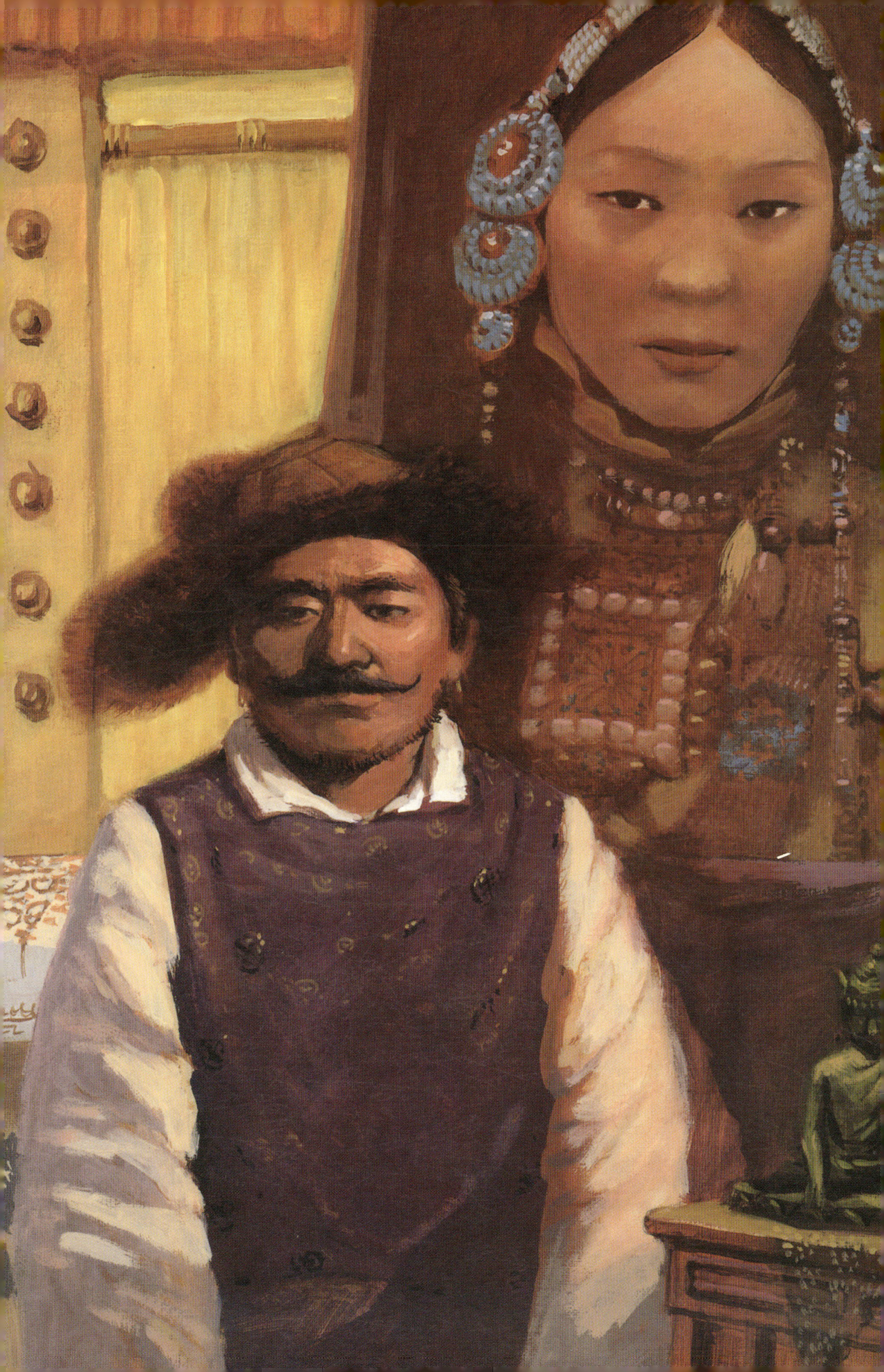

With her, she brought a statue of the Buddha. Out of love for Wen Cheng, her husband built a magnificent Buddhist temple to house this statue.

His Nepalese wife, Princess Bhrikuti Devi, also brought a statue of the Buddha to her marriage. Another beautiful temple was built for this statue. The Tibetan people began calling Wen Cheng "Gyasa," and Bhrikuti "Belsa." Together, these queens turned the heart of their husband toward the Buddha. He built many temples, and Buddhism spread throughout the land.

Several centuries later, a Tibetan lama, or Buddhist monk, travelled to meet the Mongolian king, Altan Khan. This lama, Sonam Gyatso, was known throughout Tibet for his knowledge and wisdom. The Tibetans saw him as a special holy man. They believed his soul was the soul of a man who was a dear friend of the Buddha when he was alive.

Altan Khan admired and respected Sonam Gyatso. In front of his people, he gave him the title Dalai Lama, which means Ocean of Wisdom.

The audience cheered the Dalai Lama. According to legend, flowers showered down from the skies when the Dalai Lama spoke. His listeners accepted the flowers as a sign of the Buddha's joy.

The title Dalai Lama was passed from Sonam Gyatso to many generations of lamas down to the present day. Over time, the man holding the title of Dalai Lama became the ruler of Tibet. He was leader of both the religion and the country.

The Buddhist religion teaches the belief of reincarnation. This means that when a person dies, the soul is reborn into another body. Although the body dies, the soul lives through many lifetimes in many different bodies.

Buddhists in Tibet believe that wise lamas can choose the bodies into which their souls will be reborn. In these new lives, they continue to teach and lead the

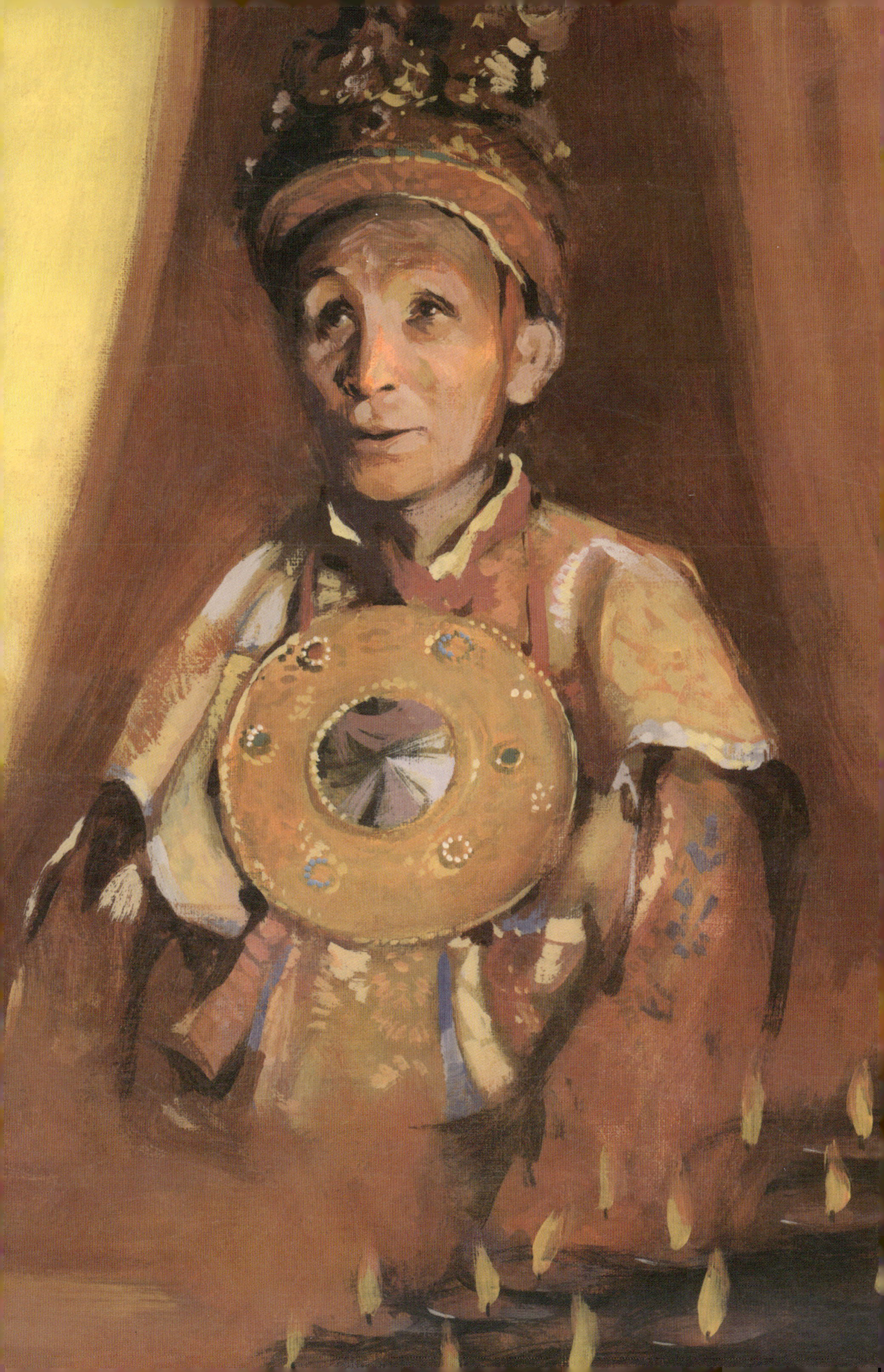

Tibetan people. Searching for the babies who have the souls of these lamas is an important task in Tibet.

In this way, each new Dalai Lama has been chosen. Whenever a Dalai Lama died, a lama with special powers would come to the temple in Lhasa, the capital city of Tibet and home of the Dalai Lama. These lamas were oracles, people who could talk to the Buddhas, who were very wise spirits. Through an oracle, the people could learn the wishes of the Buddhas.

Dressed in thick, heavy clothes and carrying a sword, the oracle would walk with his head thrown back and his neck straining forward. He would enter a magical trance. At these times, monks would write down everything the oracle said.

The monks examined the sayings of the oracle. They looked for signs in nature and tried to understand dreams. Like fitting together the pieces of a puzzle, they gathered all the clues before setting off on their search for the young child who would be the new Dalai Lama.

The Thirteenth Dalai Lama, Thubten Gyatso, died at the Potala Palace in Lhasa in 1933. Left with no leader, the monks knew they must begin the search for the sacred baby who was the reborn Dalai Lama. The Thirteenth Dalai Lama helped by leaving them a clue. After his death, his head turned to face the northeast. From this sign, the monks knew that the baby would be found somewhere to the northeast of Lhasa.

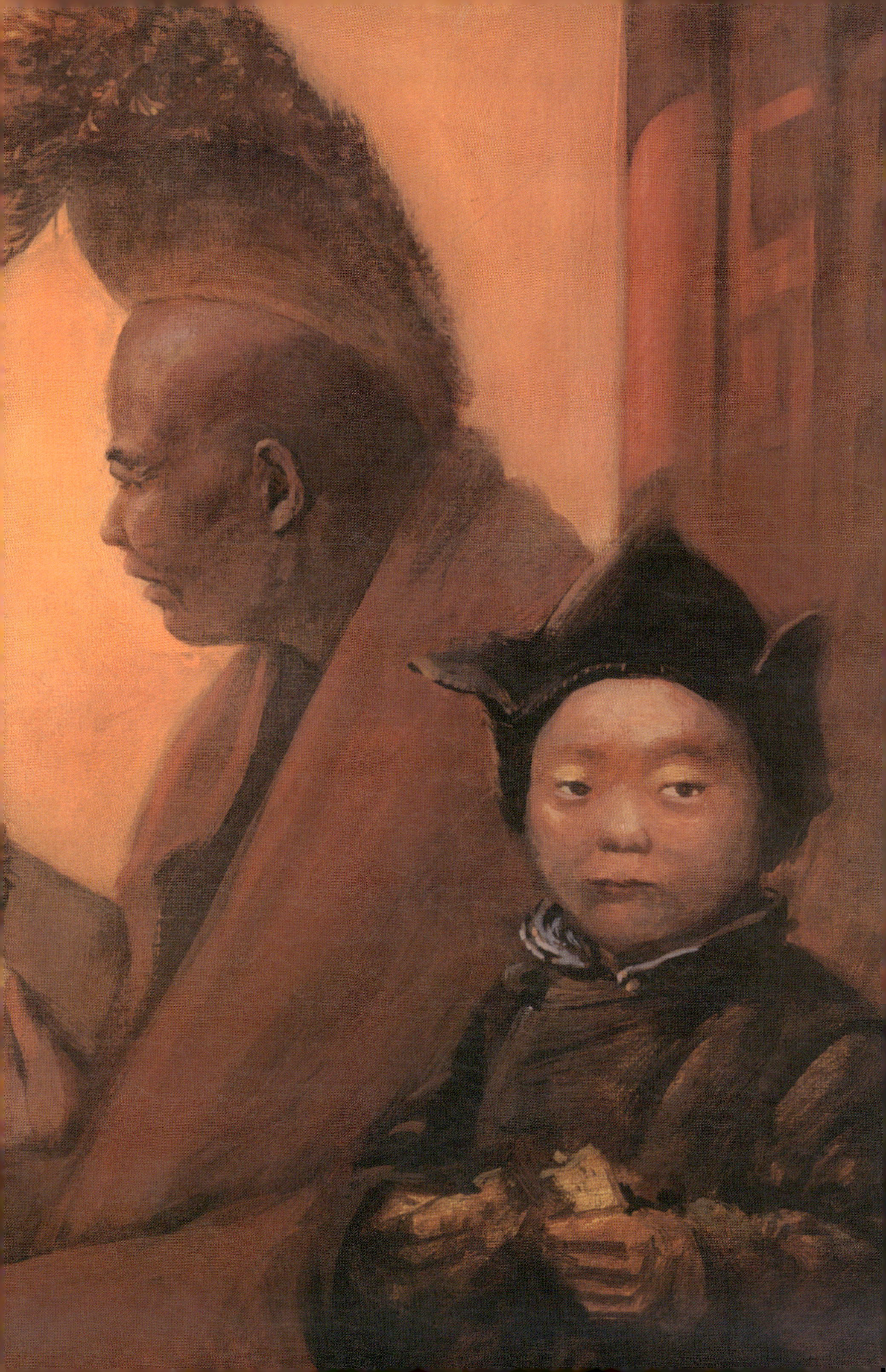

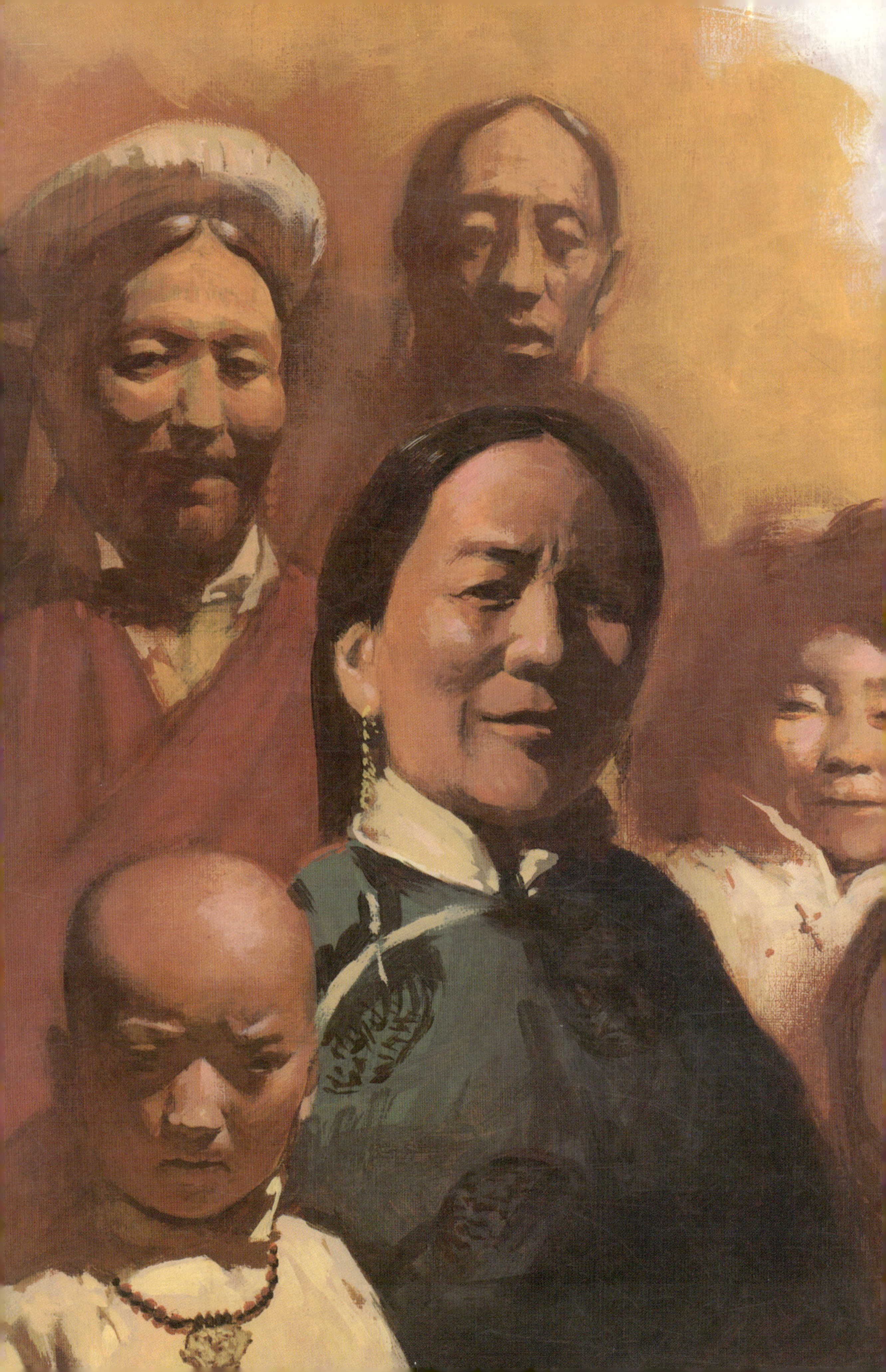

The man who was in charge of Tibet until the new Dalai Lama could take over was called the regent. His name was Reting Rinpoche. He travelled to a sacred lake to pray for help in finding the right child. An image appeared to him. He saw a monastery with a gold and green roof. A path led from the monastery to a rundown house with a turquoise roof.

Using these clues, groups of lamas began to search the country, hoping to find the sacred baby. At first, the search was disappointing. The lamas found many boys who were the right age, but none passed the special tests to prove that he was the reborn Dalai Lama. One little boy even ran away in tears.

The lamas shook their heads and sighed. They needed to come up with another way to locate the baby. When they returned to Lhasa empty-handed, all of Tibet cried out in sorrow.

In the meantime, a boy named Lhamo Dhondrub was born in the small village of Taktser in northeastern Tibet on 6 July, 1935. He was his parents' fifth child, and they realised right away that he was different from their other children.

He loved all people and animals. He seemed to understand the feelings of all creatures, even a cow, a chicken or a small flower. He hated to see anything suffer.

One monk was not discouraged in his search for the baby. Lama Kewtsang Rinpoche led a group of lamas in searching northeast of Lhasa. One day in 1937, he saw a house that matched the vision Reting Rinpoche had seen at the lake. It was Lhamo's house. By this time, he was two and a half years old.

When the lamas arrived at Lhamo's house, they were disturbed to find it was an ordinary peasant home. They wondered whether the Dalai Lama could possibly have been born in such a crude, out-of-the-way place.

They visited the home several times to test Lhamo. When trying to find a reborn lama, monks quiz the children to see whether they remember a past life as that lama. They see whether the child can recognise things that belonged to the lama. They ask questions to discover whether the child remembers things the lama did.

Kewtsang Rinpoche had brought along a number of things that belonged to the Thirteenth Dalai Lama when he was alive. Lhamo recognised a set of prayer beads right away. He took it, saying, "This is mine." He acted as if he knew them, even though he had never seen them before.

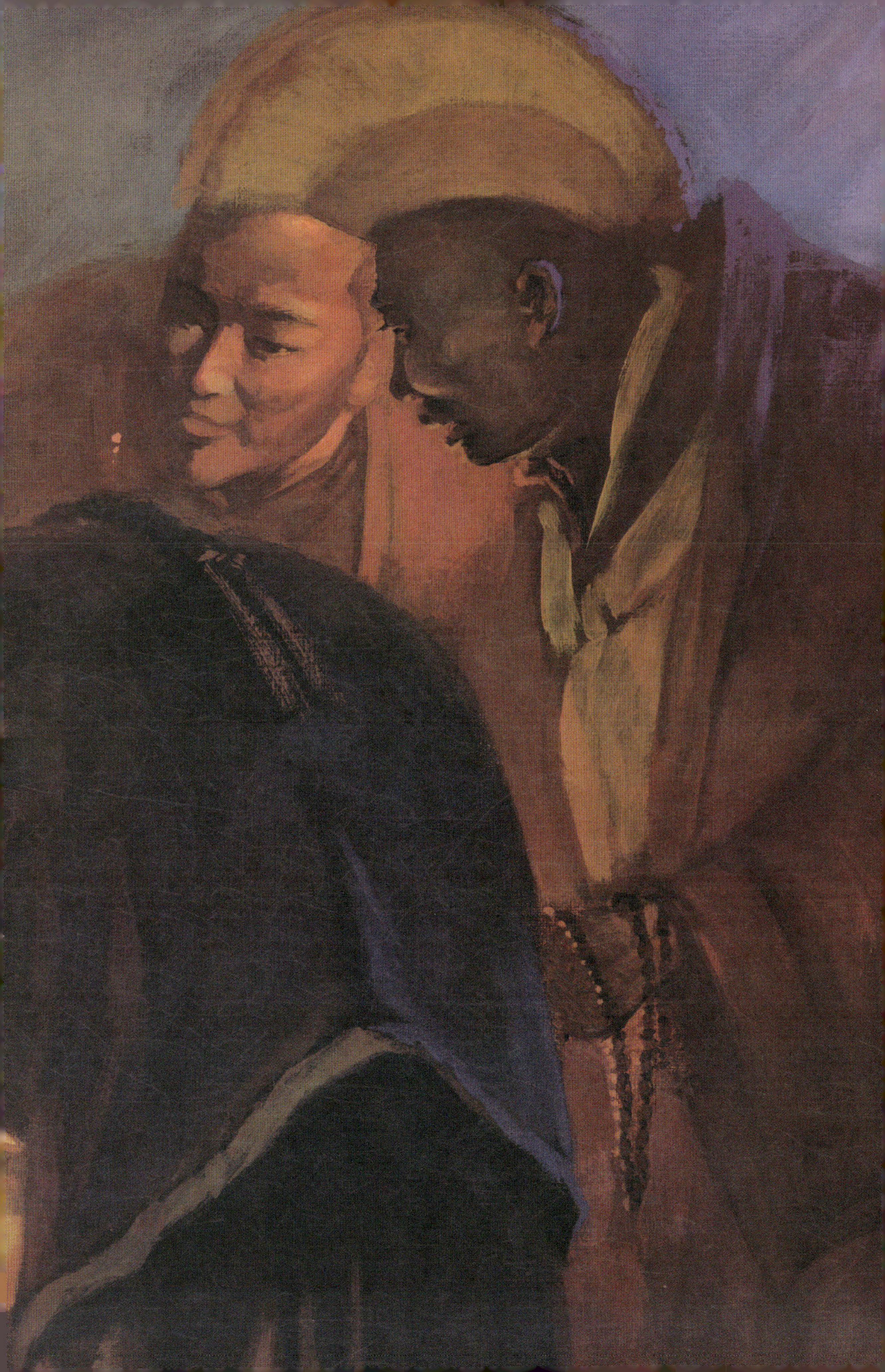

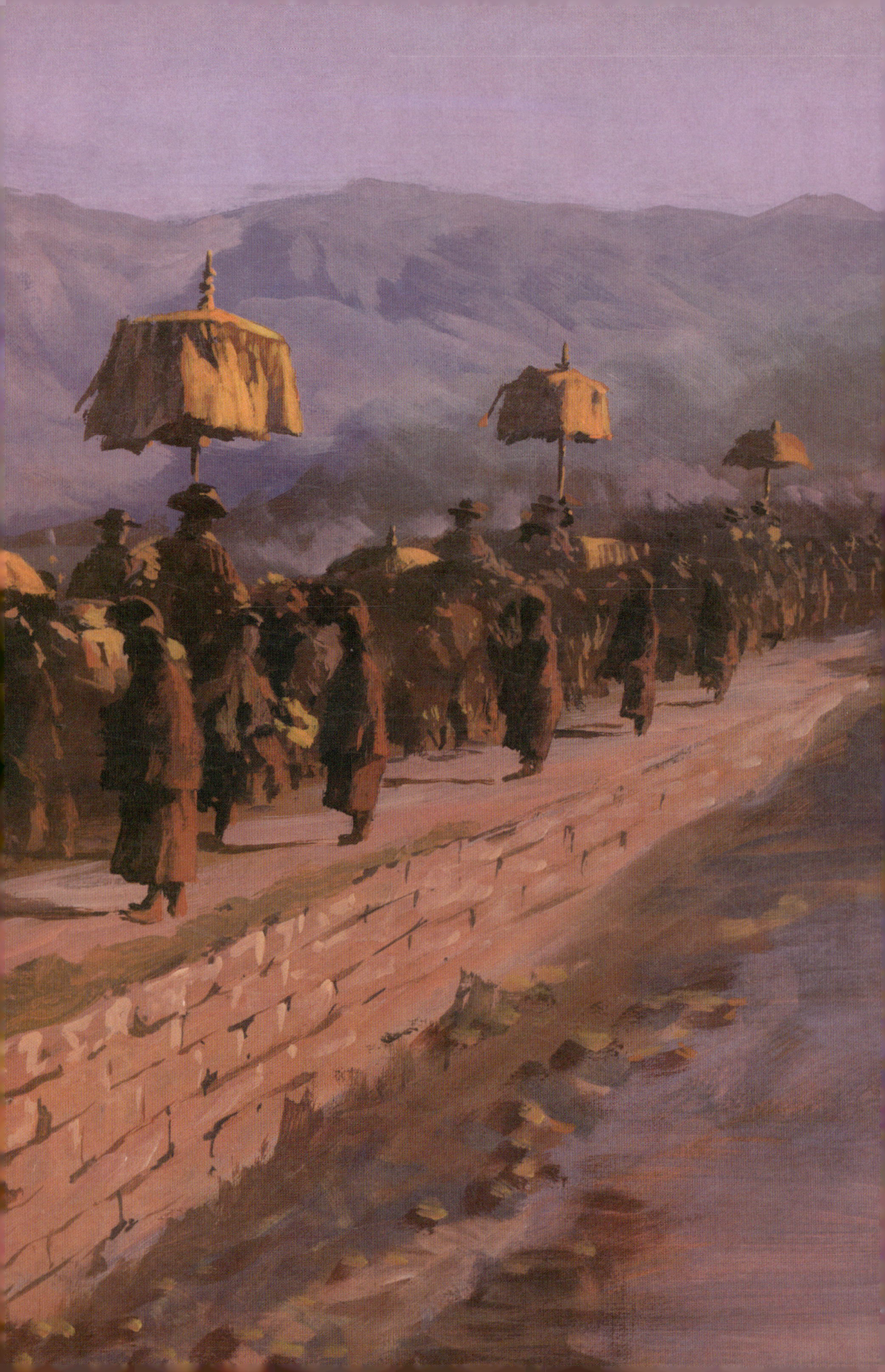

The lamas cried out in joy, "We've found him!" After searching for more than two years, Kewtsang Rinpoche and his helpers had finally found the Fourteenth Dalai Lama.

They brought Lhamo and his family to the Potala Palace in Lhaso. The journey took them halfway across Tibet. Lhamo and his family rode in sedan chairs, carried by servants. Lhamo was a typical little boy, squirming and playing with his brother while they travelled. At one point, he almost tipped over the sedan chair. He enjoyed the trip, gazing in wonder at grasslands and mountains filled with yaks, deer and horses.

They finally entered Lhasa by boat, travelling along the river. The magnificent Potala Palace rose like a giant before them. This beautiful temple, reaching up to the sky, would be Lhamo's home. Here, he would take the throne as the Fourteenth Dalai Lama.

The people of Lhasa had transformed the city to greet the sacred child. They had scrubbed every street and alley clean. The rooftop of every home was decorated with coloured banners. The crowds welcomed Lhamo with a stately ceremony. The sounds were overwhelming as huge suona horns, leather drums and bronze cymbals sang out the people's joy. The long horns made a deep sound that could be heard all over Lhasa.

People lined the road hoping to catch a glimpse of this special little boy. Little Lhamo came from a small village. He had never seen so many people before in his life. He felt a bit nervous. But, at the same time, he felt comfortable in Lhasa, as if he had been there before.

Inside the temple, the lamas greeted Lhamo with warmth and respect. They dressed him in a traditional yellow robe, and he climbed to the monastery to meet with Reting Rinpoche. The regent cut Lhamo's hair,

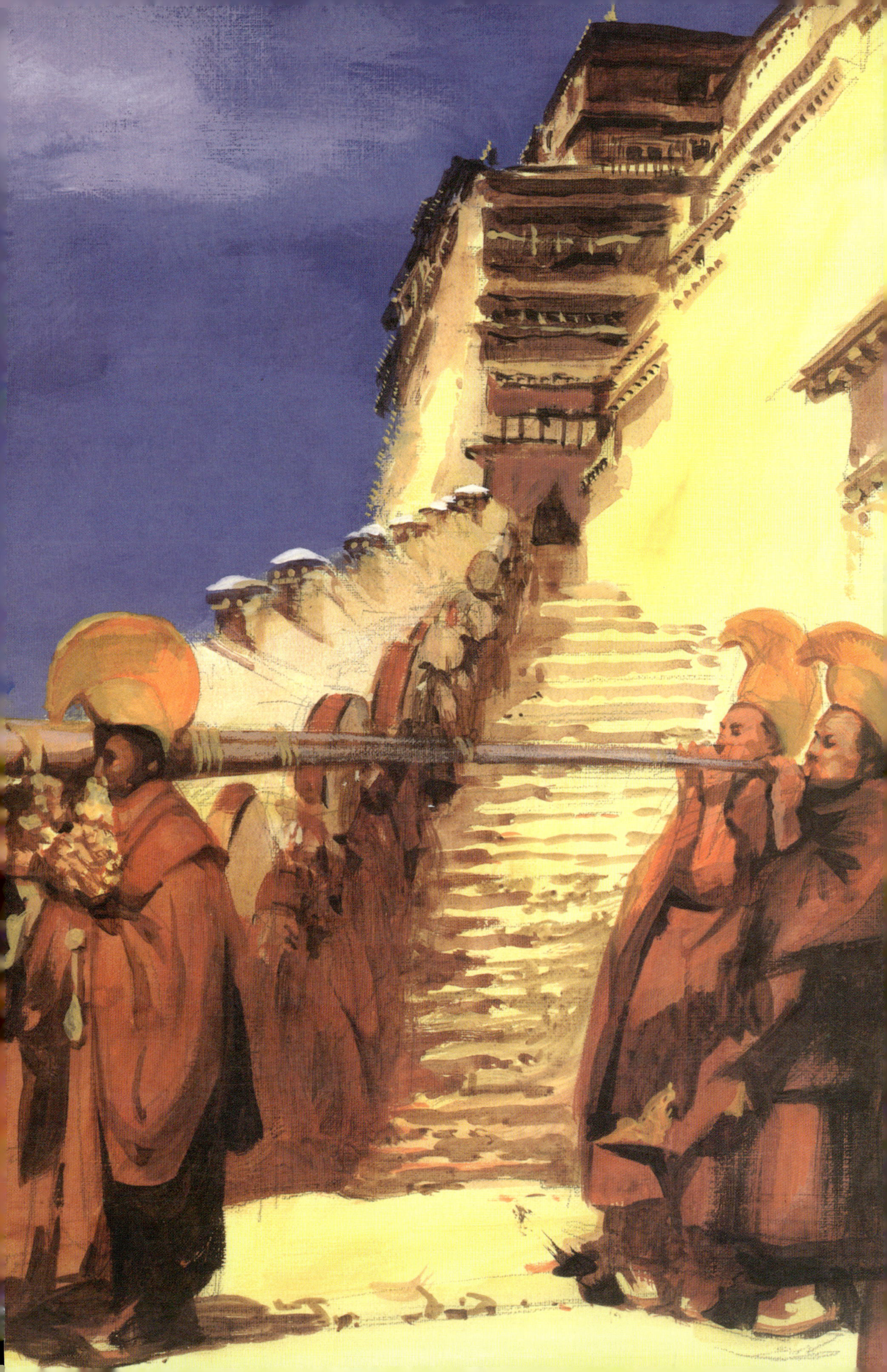

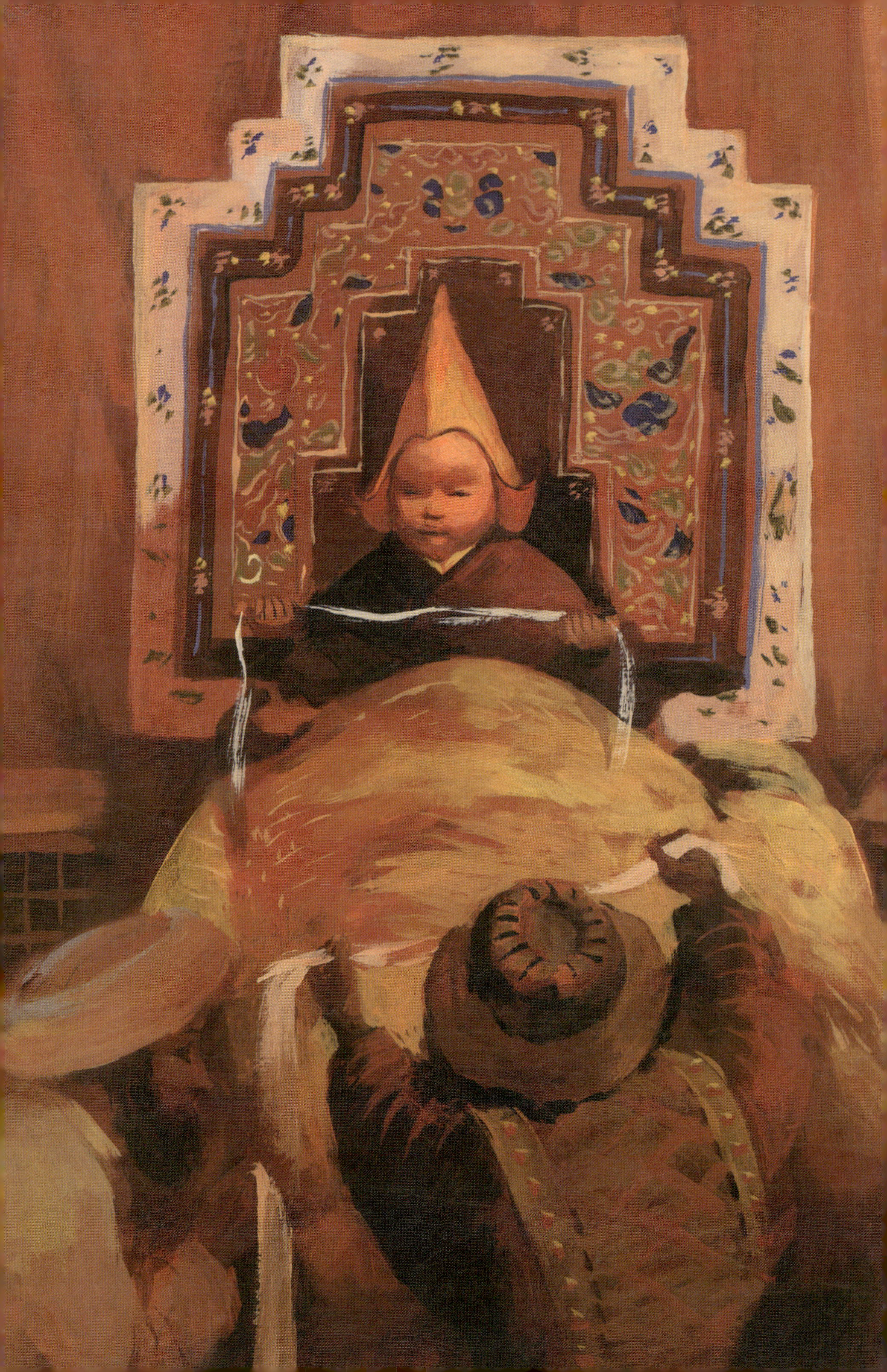

saying to him, "From now on, you will go by the name Tenzin Gyatso, the Fourteenth Dalai Lama." Tenzin means Defender of the Faith, and Gyatso means Ocean of Wisdom. Most Tibetans simply address him as "Kundun," which means "The Presence." People in Western countries call him His Holiness.

The Fourteenth Dalai Lama was still a young boy with much to learn before he could lead his country. He spent many years studying Buddhism and the Tibetan language. He also learned astronomy, the study of the stars, and geography, the study of the earth.

He sometimes had to meet with visitors from other countries. Those who met him always left with a lasting memory of his kind, gentle spirit. It was the custom for visitors to give the Dalai Lama white scarves called *katas*. In Tibet, these white scarves are offered as a greeting. They are a sign of the giver's respect and good intentions. The visitors gave the Dalai Lama their katas and asked for his blessing in return.

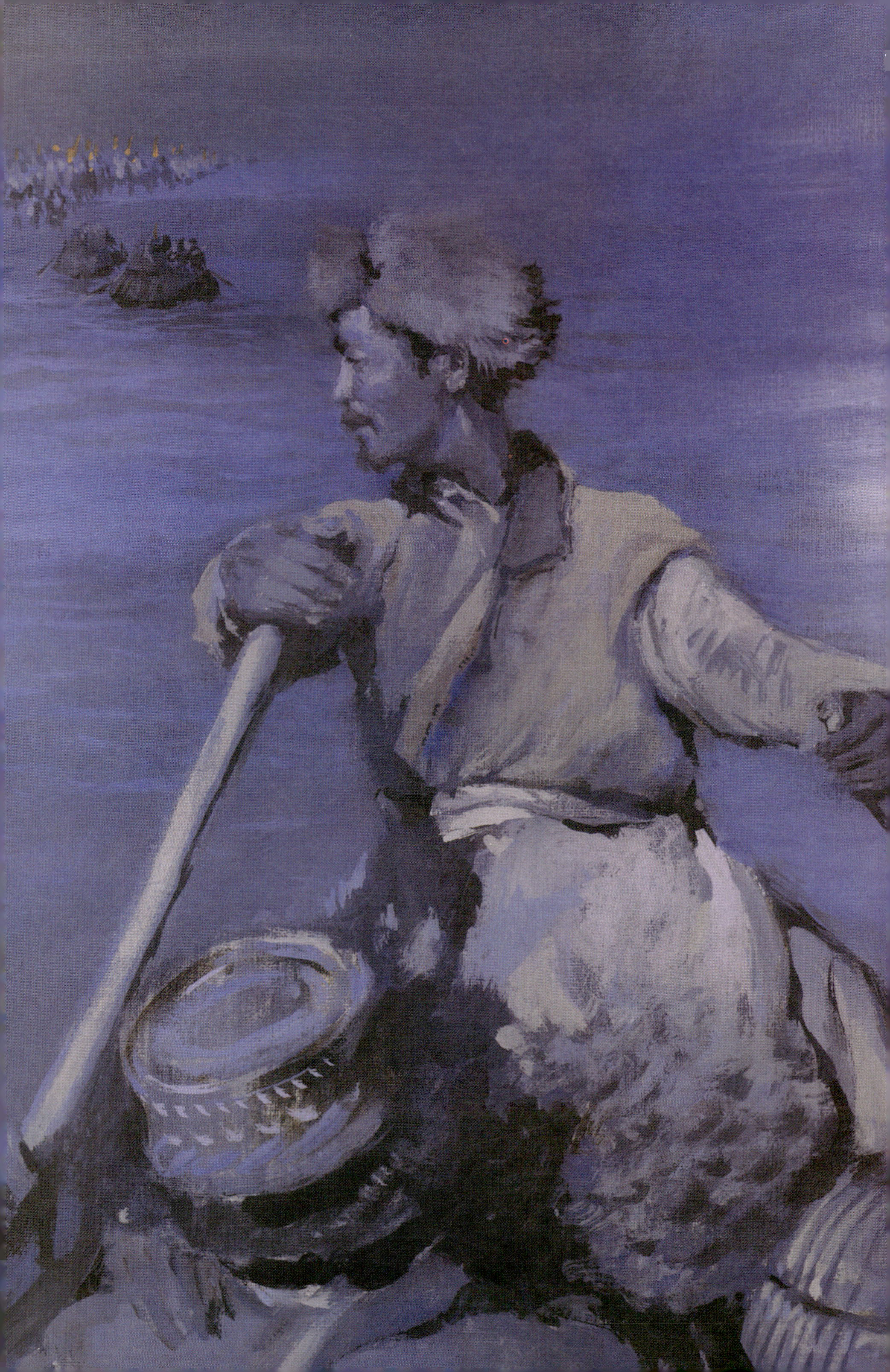

In 1949, communists gained control of China. They made plans to take over neighbouring Tibet. At this point, the Dalai Lama was only 14 years old. Normally he would not be ready take control of his country's government for several more years. But the crisis changed his situation, and he quickly took on Tibet's leadership in 1950.

The Dalai Lama tried to talk to the Chinese leaders, asking them to leave Tibet in peace. It was not to be. China did not stop threatening Tibet. In 1959, the people of Lhasa protested, speaking out against the Chinese. The Chinese army invaded Tibet and tried to make the Tibetan people give up their religion and live as communists.

The Dalai Lama puzzled over what to do next. He did not believe in fighting, and there was no way that Tibet could hold off the whole Chinese army. He knew his only choice was to leave.

The Chinese would never let him leave the country alive, so he had to steal away. On a foggy night, the Dalai Lama, his family and his helpers left the Potala Palace dressed as ordinary people. They quietly crossed the Lhasa River in small boats, fearful that guards from the Chinese army camp on the other side would spot them.

At this moment, a sudden sandstorm blew up. The Chinese guards were too busy protecting their eyes, ears and mouths from the sand to notice the Dalai Lama and his followers escaping. The sandstorm helped them to pass by many groups of Chinese soldiers unnoticed.

Their road out of Tibet was full of hardship. They had to cross high mountains and brave extreme cold. The Dalai Lama became sick, but he wasn't worried about himself. He couldn't tear his mind away from his people still living in Tibet. He worried about what would happen to them under the Chinese.

Several months after their escape, the Dalai Lama and his followers reached India. The Indian government decided to help them and let them live in India. There, they found a warm welcome from the Indian people, who admired the Dalai Lama's courage and wisdom. When the Dalai Lama passed through the streets of India riding on an elephant, thousands of people flocked to him, scattering flower petals in his path. He heard them cry, "Welcome, Dalai Lama! Long live the Dalai Lama!"

The Dalai Lama was very grateful to India and its people. He could see that they were poor, but they had helped him. And they went on helping people who fled from Tibet after him.

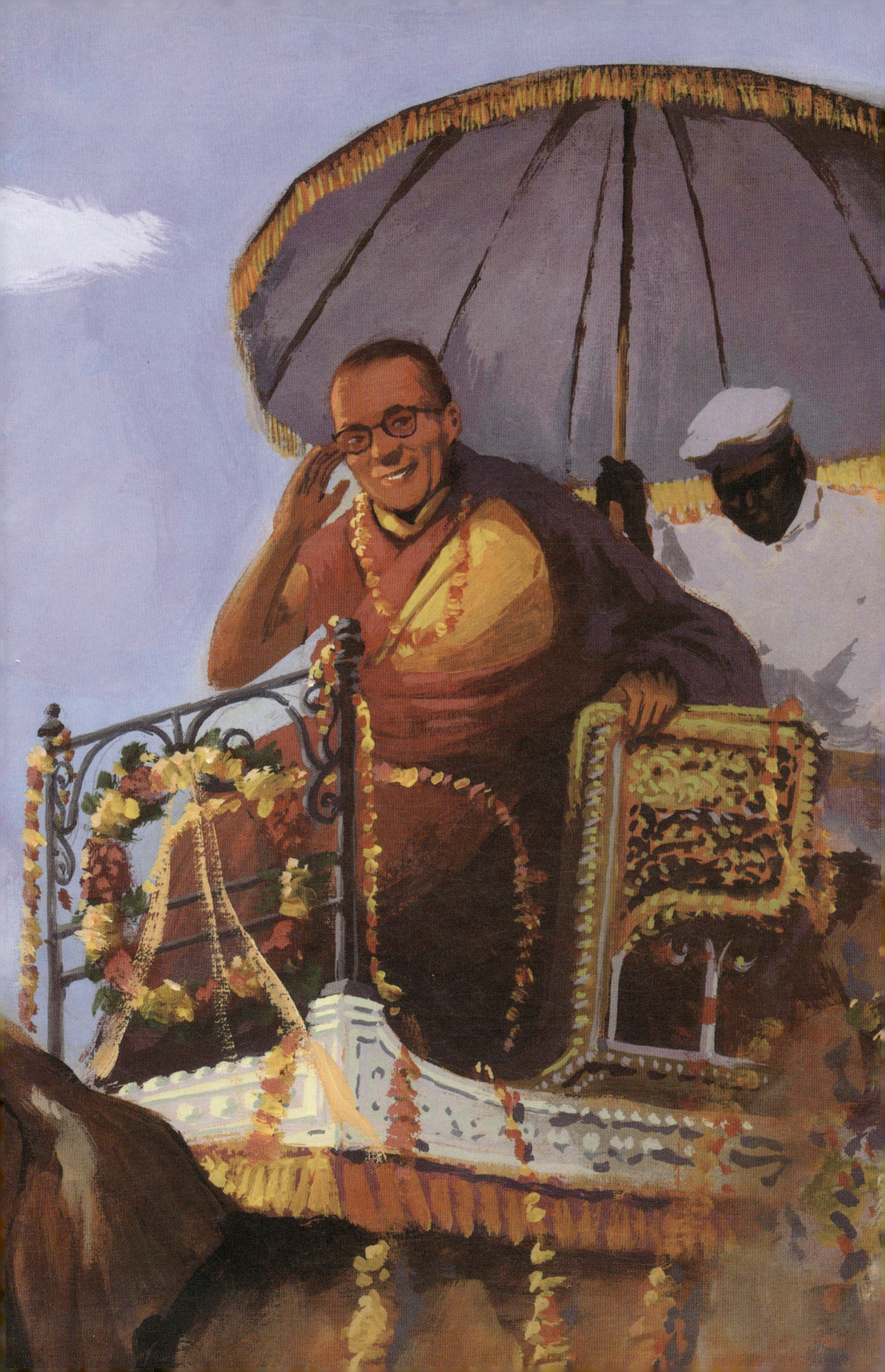

The Dalai Lama set up a government for Tibet in the town of Dharamsala in the mountains of India. It is known as the government-in-exile. Many people had to leave Tibet, and he worked to help them make new homes. Wanting to keep Tibet's religion and culture alive, he opened Tibetan schools and monasteries in India. Today, India is home to 120,000 people from Tibet.

In 1963, the Dalai Lama helped write a new constitution for the government-in-exile. He believes strongly that people should be able to choose their own government and hopes that Tibet will be a free democracy some day. The government in exile is a democracy with a parliament elected by Tibetan refugees all over the world. The constitution states that if two out of three Tibetans vote to take away the Dalai Lama's power, he has to give up his leadership. The Dalai Lama has also said that he will not be a political leader anymore if Tibet becomes free again.

After his escape, the Dalai Lama called on the world to help Tibet. No other country wanted to fight China for the sake of Tibet. But the Dalai Lama still wanted to learn more about the rest of the world. He hoped that understanding people who live in the West would help Tibet become a modern country. He also wanted to help the rest of the world understand Tibet's people, culture and problems.

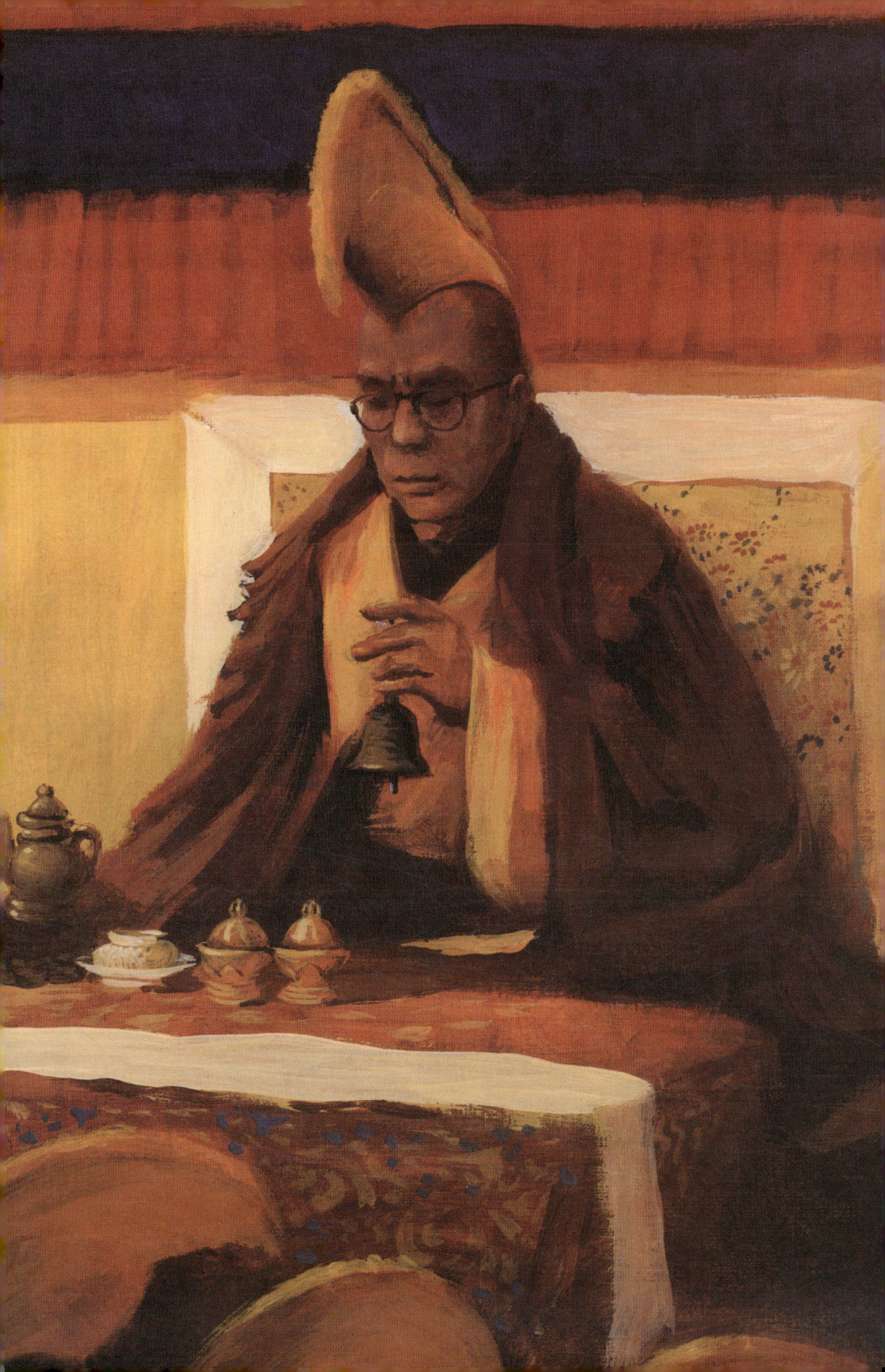

The Dalai Lama first visited Europe, then the United States. In these places, he found that he was admired and respected as a brave leader. The people seemed very curious about Tibet and asked him countless questions.

Many Europeans and Americans were deeply moved by the Dalai Lama. His wisdom, his modesty and his kind heart reached out to them. He encouraged his listeners to look for peace in their own hearts and to keep trying to win freedom for the Tibetan people in peaceful ways. Westerners who felt drawn to his message have tried to be generous toward the Tibetan people. There are now offices working to help Tibet in Europe and the United States.

The Dalai Lama has enjoyed reaching out to the West. Together with his disciples around the world, he prays for world peace. In 1989, the Dalai Lama was invited to Norway to accept the Nobel Prize for Peace.

He told the audience, "It is an honor and pleasure to be among you today. I speak to you as just another human being; as a simple monk.

"As a free spokesperson for my captive countrymen and -women, I feel it is my duty to speak out on their behalf," he continued. "The awarding of this prize to me, a simple monk from faraway Tibet, fills us Tibetans with hope. It means we have not been forgotten. Reason, courage, determination and the desire for freedom can ultimately win. That is a source of hope not only for us Tibetans, but for all oppressed people."

As His Holiness delivered his speech, the faces of the world's poor suddenly appeared in his mind's eye. He had been wondering what to do with the money that came with the Nobel Prize. Now he knew. He would divide the money, giving it to people with leprosy in India, hungry people throughout the world and his own suffering Tibetan people.

The Dalai Lama continues to speak for the Tibetan people and their struggle. He wrote a peace plan, but China did not accept it. "There will be everlasting peace only when human rights are taken seriously, when the people are no longer hungry and when the people and the state are free," he has said.

His Holiness has said that he will not choose to be reborn in a country that is under Chinese control. If Tibet is not freed in his lifetime, he will be reborn somewhere else. Each lifetime is supposed to build on the last. He has already escaped from the Chinese in this life.

Should Tibet be freed while he is still alive, the Dalai Lama has said he will not be the ruler of a free Tibet. He feels that the Tibetan people should be free to decide their own future.

The road ahead is still very uncertain for the Dalai Lama. Will the Fourteenth Dalai Lama be the last? Only time will tell. But the kindness, wisdom and strength that the Dalai Lama has shown in his struggle for freedom, human rights and world peace will never be forgotten. "Peace starts with each one of us," he tells us. "When we have inner peace, we can be at peace with those around us."

BIOGRAPHY

Author Anne Marie Sullivan received her Bachelor of Arts degree in English from Temple University. She has worked in the publishing field as a writer and editor. She lives with her husband and three children in a Philadelphia suburb.